Employer Branding

Case studies and comments from industry professionals

Edited by

Hugh Davies and Susan Moir

Author: Davies, Hugh
Title: Employer Branding, Case studies and comments from industry professionals
ISBN: 978-1-742841-34-2 (pbk.)

Published by Book Pal
www.bookpal.com.au

CONTENTS

Foreword

My research over the last decade into employer branding in the UK, Europe and Australia has led me to define an employer brand as *a generalised recognition for being known among key stakeholders for providing a high quality employment experience, and a distinctive organizational identity which employees value, engage with and feel confident and happy to promote to others*. Employer branding refers to the process by which branding concepts and marketing, communications and HR techniques are applied to create this generalised recognition.

Until quite recently, most practitioners working in this field have focused on the attraction of new talent, largely because of the 'talent wars' that characterised much of the 1990s and millennium until the onset of the global financial crisis in 2007-8. So employer branding became associated with the external labour market application of marketing and communications tools (e.g. recruitment advertising, publicity, events) to attracting potential employees. Even then this external branding of the organization in labour markets always rested on having existing employees 'live the brand' because of their potential influence on customers and potential employees. With the onset of recession and a sovereign debt crisis in many countries, the focus on employer branding gradually shifted to improving levels of employee engagement, arguably an even more important role given the potential returns on getting the maximum payback from often heavy investments in human and social capital.

While the importance of talent attraction and engagement make employer branding a serious contender for inclusion in any list of high performance work practices, I also believe that employer branding can play a strategic role in 'future-proofing' corporate reputations, arguably a bigger agenda. Corporate reputation management attempts to reconcile an organization's needs to compete strategically by being *different* from competitors while remaining *socially legitimate* by securing a generalised recognition for providing high quality goods and services. Few executives would disagree that reputation management has become one of the key long term issues for all organizations as the recent banking crisis in America and Europe and disasters such as Deepwater Horizon oil spill had on BPs share price and worldwide reputation have shown. Thus reputational capital is widely seen as one of the most valuable intangible resources with significant effects on a firm's performance. In turn, reputational capital helps organizations compete in global markets for customers, talent, finance, business partners and other resources. So employer branding has a central role to play not just in HRM but in creating and protecting *reputational capital* by facilitating *wealth creation* through innovation, *wealth protection and wealth distribution*, which are the three aims of good corporate governance.

Seen in this light, employer branding has moved on from its early associations with recruitment and communications, although these remain core issues for organizations and employer branding specialists. So I am pleased to see a group of Australian practitioners from different backgrounds taking the subject seriously in a variety of ways, tackling some of the bigger strategic issues as well as the traditional concerns. Each contribution from a range of Australian organizations adds significantly to our understanding of different aspects of employer branding in practice and together they represent a serious attempt to provide an overall guide and route map to this important field for HR, branding and communications staff who seek to know more about it.

It is indeed gratifying to see reflective practitioners take the time to think and write about their work in a lively and informed way, which I'm sure, will reward anyone who takes the time to read this new book.

Professor Graeme Martin
(University of Glasgow Business School, Scotland)
Graeme Martin, PhD, is Professor of HRM at the University of Glasgow Business School and has written, researched and consulted extensively into employer branding over the last decade in a number of countries. He is a regular visitor to Australia and you can find out more about him at http://www.gla.ac.uk/schools/business/staff/graememartin/

Introduction

What brings talent in to an organisation? What makes good people stay? These are simple questions but ones that we discuss often with our clients. These may seem like "soft" attributes and of little consequence, but an employer brand, and the culture experienced by employees are very much things that matter in the business of attracting and keeping good people.

The idea for this short book arose in discussion with one of our client firms. It gathered speed and quickly developed into a real project of interest as we engaged other clients. It seems that right now increasing numbers of Human Resources professionals, senior line managers and partners in professional services firms are interested in the importance of the employer brand their organisation has, or should have, in the context of talent attraction and retention.

This book is a collection of short chapters by representatives of a number of large organisations active in Australia and elsewhere. It also includes perspectives of experts in the field and those supplying services to organisations relating to employer branding. It comprises a mixture of perspectives drawn from people at the coalface in this area.

The book captures the words and thoughts of a range of quite different people and organisations. The chapters are written in different styles, with different voices – but this brings authenticity in the perspectives of those involved.

There are some broad questions to consider as you read what follows:

- What is an "employer brand"? How is this different from the wider organisational brand presented in relation to products and services, or to the reputation and "brand" presented to shareholders?

- How is an employer brand built?

- How is an employer brand conveyed to people considering joining an organisation? And how is it conveyed to current employees to build their engagement and commitment?

- What happens to an employer brand when disaster strikes an organisation's broader "corporate" brand, and what should be done in this circumstance?

- How might a good employer brand be affected and/or retained during times when a restructure and downsizing might be needed?

- What might be needed if two organisations, with existing strong brands, join together to create a new entity?

We believe an employer brand is critical to the attraction of talented people, and to the retention of good people. We think an employer brand flows and is built through a number of activities and practices. It is experienced through a number of channels, and increasingly through the emerging social media. But let's see what you think after reading the short essays which make up this book.

Who are "we" by the way?

Together with my colleagues, I lead a boutique career transition and career development services firm, headquartered in Melbourne but operating across Australia. We work with senior people: Chief Executives, Partners and senior executives - who typically are facing a need to transition to new careers beyond their organisations, or who need to address development opportunities or career shifts of significance within their organisations. We all find working with individuals at significant career turning points richly rewarding. Another source of enthusiasm for us is in our research: we do invest in building new insights in this area.

This book is an example of "collaborative research". We don't set ourselves up as experts in employer branding. Here our aim was to work with others to try to become much better informed in an area of joint interest.

I would like to pay tribute to those who have contributed to this book. They include Susan Moir and Norah Breekveldt in Macfarlan Lane, Colin Jasper, Lisa Hart, Chris Lokum, Brie Macklin, Peter Brydon, Jenny Gillam, Tim Grogan, Anand Rego, Sharon Tan, Geraldine Coy, Alison McLeod, Jim Bailey and Professor Graeme Martin – who kindly agreed to write our foreword. In some instances, these individuals have "put themselves out there", acknowledging challenges in their organisations and working hard to provide leadership in an area not always well understood or given particular support.

We hope you will enjoy this material, and recommend it to others. Any profits after cost recoveries will be given to Big Brothers Big Sisters: a great organisation in the work it does for young people in need of adult "brothers" and "sisters".

Hugh Davies
Macfarlan Lane

Accidents Happen. But not if you can help it.

Building the employer brand of WorkSafe Victoria

Geraldine Coy

The organisation

The Victorian WorkCover Authority, trading as WorkSafe Victoria, is a statutory authority of the state government of Victoria, Australia. Our Mission is "Working with the community to deliver outstanding workplace safety, together with quality care and insurance protection to workers and employers."

The scheme is funded by Victorian employers who pay a percentage of their total remuneration which provides the insurance cover.

"Victorian workers returning home safe every day".

This simple statement did not happen by accident. Rather, it was the culmination and integration of many highly planned and researched activities that began in 2004.

Our brand challenge

In 2004 we knew we had serious issues with our brand in the community. And our people were telling us this in our employee opinion surveys too – in 2004 only 46% of our people agreed with the statement "WorkSafe Victoria is highly regarded by the general public".

Two things are important to remember of this time. We had an inspectorate who were wedded to their rights of enforcement under the then current legislation, and a client base who saw safety as a compliance activity at best and the inspectorate, as the face of the (then) Victorian Workcover Authority, the enforcers of that compliance. It was not a good cocktail of popular and receptive regard.

The first foundational plank was the Chris Maxwell review of the Occupational Health and Safety Act in 2004. This comprised a rewrite of the Act, (implemented with effect 1 July 2005), based on (amongst other legislative reforms), significant behavioural change required by the regulator in the conduct of our business, particularly in the interface between our Health and Safety Inspectorate and our clients - Employers, Workers, Health and Safety Representatives. Essentially this required the inspectors to interact with our clients in an educative, enabling, advisory and guiding way in the first instance, and only then in an enforcement capacity to ensure change to safe work practices.

We began with our people

"Getting our Act Together" was the internal banner of the 2004 all employee workshops where we brought everyone together to explore how the Maxwell recommendations were to affect each of our jobs.

Uniquely, we have always known that our value differentiator in the attraction of people to our workforce, has been their almost vocational calling to serve in the interests of the community, to prevent injury and indeed, death in the workplace. We attract people who care enough to look after the interests of injured workers and the families of those who have suffered the tragic loss of one of their own. So we didn't have to work hard at getting people aligned to the mission of WorkSafe.

It was more about HOW we were going about our work which needed to change. Maxwell's review gave us the first four of our values to work towards implementation. We drew on these values to run the workshops with our employees. They gave us the language to work out how we needed to change behaviours. "From Cop to Coach" was how we defined the change to our new client promise.

Our own people surfaced the fifth value of Caring, picking up on the rehabilitation and compensation focus. The inspectorate had to undergo a recertification and licensing process. By the time the new Act was implemented in July 2005, we had a workforce fully aligned to a new way of doing business and built around our values:

- We are Constructive in the way we provide information, advice and services.
- We are Accountable for what we do and what we say. We live up to our promises.
- We work in a Transparent way in an environment which is open and honest.

- We are Effective by working collaboratively to deliver high quality services.
- We demonstrate Care by showing empathy in our dealings with everyone we work with.

Taking it to the public

The second foundational plank was launched in 2006 with a bold campaign to elevate the importance of Safety in the minds of all Victorians. We sought to change attitudes, and to drive change with an emotional appeal. We recognised that the most important reason for being safe at work, was not at work at all. At its most basic, the proposition was that people need to be safe at work to enjoy the things that are really important in our lives outside of work – family and friends. Therefore, the television commercial, associated communications materials and subsequent campaigns in the series do not feature people working, nor do they feature a workplace.

The core idea was encapsulated in the line 'The most important reason for making your workplace safe is not at work at all'. The television commercial featuring people returning home from work to 'their most important reason for workplace safety', with a dash of tension around whether all the 'homecomers' would return safely.

The campaign generated unprecedented discussion and media comment in the community and succeeded in its aim of elevating the importance of safety at work. Discussion of the campaign (particularly the television commercial) was high, including talkback radio, newspaper column space and in the public's correspondence with WorkSafe.

Findings from Sweeney Research confirmed that the message had resonated with WorkSafe's key audiences and that message delivery was on the mark. Importantly, significant actions had resulted from the campaign. The research found that 93% of employers and 85% of employees were aware of the campaign. High approval percentages were registered around the campaign, recognising the value of relationships outside the workplace.

The campaign resonated not only in Victoria, but across Australia (it has been adopted in six other states, and in Washington State, USA!) on an unparalleled level, evidenced in overwhelming community support and continues to drive positive actions in the workplace every day.

And then back to our employees again

Our own employees' responses to how proud they felt to be a part of the change began to show in EOS results. In 2010 85% of our people said they agreed that WorkSafe was regarded positively by the general public…and recall that this percentage was 46% in 2004.

> *"The changes I have seen over these past 17 years….the improvement to the WorkSafe image and reputation. WorkSafe has become the key driver for Health & Safety in Victoria in the workplace and does what it advertises "to ensure all employees come home safely each day". WorkSafe has certainly become a respected and innovative leader.*

WorkSafe is a very rewarding, fulfilling, healthy and happy place to be. I treasure my job coming to work each day, to share love and information with my colleagues." Margy, Worksafe employee, 17 years service.

We have continued to build on this platform with our campaigns for improving workplace cultural norms for Supervisors and Young Workers. We have focused on driving change in thinking (and doing) about safety and rehabilitation, particularly returning workers to work. At the same time, we follow this up with a reminder to all that we are at the end of the day, a regulator, and "Inspector Max Johnson" will enforce compliance with the regulations so that we can ensure that employers meet their obligations to provide all workers with a safe workplace.

Translating this transformation into our EVP

We asked ourselves a few questions. With a newly aligned workforce behind our organisational vision and mission, how could we attract more of the right people to our workforce? And how could we better retain the good people we had on board in an increasingly competitive market for skills? Was there an equally positive and genuine reflection of values authentically delivered from inside the organisation? Were our tangible and intangible benefits and rewards authentically reflective of what we stood for in the community?

We knew that we needed to integrate the brand into our own Value Proposition in order to complete the picture for people looking into our organisation from the outside, but also for our own people looking from the organisation to outside opportunity.

We embarked upon another round of discussion groups. We listened to a cross section of employees from all of our regional and central offices, across all of our business units, diverse in age, gender and length of service.

Again, we found that our employer brand is interconnected emotionally with our value proposition.

What we stand for as an employer, (our values), our personality, (what employment experience do our people have here), and what we look like (our recruitment strategy) needed to complement and integrate with one another to realise an authenticity about WorkSafe which would ring true in the employment marketplace.

How we brought our EVP to life

We evolved an offer which we believed addresses the whole person at work in the organisation. This aim was to meet their emotional, social, financial, community and health and wellbeing needs. We worked on building the component parts of these needs in order to ensure a balanced offer which would be hard to pass up in a competitive market. We are a public sector employer and we were determined to take on the advantage and scope enjoyed by the private sector beyond our ability to attract employees on remuneration benefits alone.

Since the beginning of 2004 with the building of our **Leadership Development** program, and its launch in early

2005, we had worked on the enhancement of the employment value proposition.

Feelingood@work is the overarching umbrella for what is now a four-chapter approach to the offer:

Career and Development demonstrates our **commitment to learning and development** and career enhancement opportunities, both internally and externally.

Health and Wellbeing provides a host of **physical and emotional wellbeing** activities and interventions which our employees can access voluntarily. These are subsidised by the organisation.

Rewards and Benefits offers benefits in flexible working arrangements and financial planning. A new recognition program helps us to celebrate the achievements of our people, against measures linking back to our values and leadership goals.

Community extends our offer to employees, encouraging them to be **socially responsible.** We have an active Social club, Green Office Program, and a commitment to support community volunteering, which is integrated into our leadership development programs.

Our people loved it

Encouraged by the feedback from our discussion groups, we made a DVD of employee comments "A Great Place to Work", an unscripted and spontaneous record of how people felt about working within WorkSafe. Here are some of the quotes:

"Working for an organisation whose goal it is to promote health and safety in the workplace. It's a noble cause that everyone is involved in."

"There's a range of opportunities for everyone – physios, lawyers, accountants etc. The diversity of people is good."

"WorkSafe is focussed on people – not just with safety in the workplace but their own people being happy at work."

"A lot of training is offered in-house and externally too. You can find a degree externally and the organisation (WorkSafe) will fund it."

"The variety of programs and benefits are great. Like feelingood@work – the management here really look after their people."

We were able to evidence a real change in how we were perceived as an employer with the advent of our Graduate Program in 2006. With ten two year graduate rotations on offer each year, we are able to select the very best candidates across ten different disciplines from over 1,000 applications each year. Now, in 2011, having just completed our fifth intake, we are proud to report an 81% retention rate of our graduates.

So we took it externally

In 2009/10 we launched our much enhanced, creative and bold recruitment advertising. The advertisements were built on our confidence in an EVP which we could back and evidence.

We knew then that our employees believed that they:

- were part of a great cause,
- were part of a powerful brand,
- found their work interesting and important,
- worked for an organisation that cared about their people and
- earned good benefits too!

We needed to ensure that the experience of the applicant coming into the organisation and that of the current employees aligned with the "look and feel" of the strong EVP.

This meant a lot of remedial work. First sight for an aspirant employee of WorkSafe was to be greeted by the standard official government, pretty cardboardy applications process, and a fairly rigid, boring website and messaging response process.

So we aligned the newly designed and networked internet (and also our internal intranet) so that we deliver a consistent and true message in the gateway experience.

As part of our business partnership strategy, we continue to build and enhance a cleaner, simpler recruitment system which "fits" with the EVP, and rings true throughout the employment period.

Where we are today

At WorkSafe we can truthfully assert that our values guide us in everything we do. Our employees help to protect and improve people's lives. They feel proud of our mission and their role in delivering high quality services to the Victorian Community.

> *"I was attracted to WorkSafe because of their core mission. I really liked the idea of working in a place where I could help make a difference to society. I also assumed that WorkSafe would foster a positive work environment and really promote work-life balance to show Victorian businesses that this can be achieved. Since working at WorkSafe, the assumptions I had made were fulfilled. I work with great people who are keen to promote both my professional and personal development, and WorkSafe offers all employees a range of opportunities that encourage work-life balance. I find my work to be meaningful and fulfilling, and the environment I work in fosters productivity and openness. These are just some of the many reasons why I enjoy working for WorkSafe."* Jess, graduate program, one year in.

Our employment brand is much more than a name, slogan or set of images. It is represented by the way our people, and the people who know us well, feel and think about us. We were proud to have been presented with the Compass HR Leader Employer of Choice – Public Sector) 2010 award, and as employees, we are proud;

- of what we represent in the community - that the community trusts & respects Worksafe;
- of how we can help shape the sort of organisation this is - that continuous improvement is the norm;
- that we have the support & opportunity for self-improvement;
- of our achievements;

- that we're amongst the few that have the opportunity to work here.

Geraldine Coy,

At the time of writing, Geraldine was Executive Director Human Resources and Change Management, Worksafe, Victoria. She has since left this organisation.

Employer branding for professional service firms

Colin Jasper & Lisa Hart

"You are a bus driver. The bus, your company, is at a standstill, and it's your job to get it going. You have to decide where you're going, how you're going to get there, and who's going with you.

Most people assume that great bus drivers (read: business leaders) immediately start the journey by announcing to the people on the bus where they're going—by setting a new direction or by articulating a fresh corporate vision.

In fact, leaders of companies that go from good to great start not with "where" but with "who." They start by getting the right people on the bus, the wrong people off the bus, and the right people in the right seats."

The above quote from Jim Collins' *Good to Great* highlights the importance to organisations of attracting and retaining the right people. This is true for all organisations, including professional service firms. However - in law, accounting and other professional service firms it could be argued the need is even greater. Why? Because in these firms the people are the product. If the sole tax partner of a firm chooses to leave, the firm no longer has a tax service. If a group of partners and their teams decide to move firms, they are likely to take clients with them. Effectively the organisation loses a small business unit. It didn't sell it, or restructure it - it lost the revenue because of the inability to keep the right people "on the bus". But for those who are effective at attracting the right people, the opposite is true. They can build their firm through an effective lateral recruitment strategy. They can build their firm through acquiring small business units from other firms. *Acquiring* - without payment.

A key element of success for professional service firms (PSFs) is the ability to attract, retain and develop leading talent. This in turn attracts interesting work from leading clients and justifies a price premium. Given the importance of attracting and retaining staff to the success of PSFs you may expect they have developed great expertise in this area. Unfortunately our research does not support this. In a major study of the legal market we found that 1/3 of staff indicated they are keen to move firms in the next 12 months. If this desire were to become reality in a firm, it would devastate that firm. So what are staff seeking and what do firms need to do to improve satisfaction and loyalty?

About the study

The **Acritas Top Law Firms to Work For** survey is the world's first employer brand study to measure brand promise and brand reality on a global level in the legal sector. We aim to achieve in excess of 10,000 responses by the third year of the study. For this first pilot study, we have conducted in excess of 800 interviews from employees of more than 200 law firms and law students across a wide geographic footprint. Countries represented included Australia, Belgium, Canada, China, France, Germany, Hong Kong, India, Singapore, Spain, Turkey, the UK and the US.

The study covers:

- ✓ What employees seek from their firm
- ✓ What drives employee satisfaction and loyalty
- ✓ How satisfied employees are with the law firms they currently work for
- ✓ Which firms are perceived to be the best by those currently and potentially working within the legal sector, and
- ✓ What is important to law students when seeking future employment?

What's important to employees?

What do professionals value? What is it that drives staff loyalty? Is it the perception of the firm's standing in the market, the quality of the service provided to clients or the relationships they have with their colleagues? Are they seeking an environment where they can develop or an opportunity to fast track their career? What role does remuneration play and how important is work-life balance?

The study had employees assess their firm's performance on 26 separate questions. Analysis of these questions highlighted five distinct factors that drive staff satisfaction and loyalty, namely:

- The clarity of the firm's vision
- The quality of the work
- The opportunity and recognition received
- The support received, and
- Work / life balance.

Clarity of the firm's vision

Employees want to know and understand the vision and ambition of the firm. They wish to understand what focus the firm places on clients, staff and financial results and the relationship between these. The firm's vision should not be the secret business of management and partners but needs to be shared with all employees. Employees want to know that the firm has a vision and want to feel proud of that vision. Simply sharing the vision creates an openness that is valued by staff.

The quality of the work

Staff want to be proud of the quality of the work the firm performs. This includes the quality of the people they work with, the quality of the client base and the reputation the firm enjoys in the marketplace. It also includes the nature of the work they undertake and the opportunity they have for personal interaction with clients.

The opportunity and recognition received

The third factor is the opportunity to develop and progress their career. This includes receiving clear direction on what is expected, and appropriate feedback on performance. It also includes recognition, reward and remuneration that is appropriate given the contribution. Staff want to feel valued and see that they have the opportunity to progress within the firm.

The support received

Another factor relates to how supported staff feel they are in their roles. While the previous factor is about the future, this factor is about the here and now. Do they get the support they need from their manager? Do they get the training they need to do their job? How collaborative is the firm and do they get the assistance they need from support departments. In short, is the firm helping staff to do their jobs effectively?

Work / life balance

The final factor relates to the ability to balance work, with life outside the office. This factor has been a challenge for many PSFs. Firms with a strong ethos of client service are often quite overt in their expectation that if the client wants the work done, staff are expected to do whatever it takes to deliver - often in very short timeframes. Other firms view staff as the factory that creates the product for sale. By driving the factory harder, they can increase profits. While client satisfaction and profitability are important to the ongoing viability of a firm, achieving these outcomes in this manner needs to be balanced against employee satisfaction and loyalty.

While not all five factors are equally important to all employees, they are the key components that drive staff satisfaction and loyalty.

What drives satisfaction and loyalty?

Not surprisingly the primary driver of pride in the firm is ***the quality of the work***. Where staff believe the firm delivers in the market and is recognised accordingly, they indicate they are proud to work for the firm. This is also the primary driver for being willing to recommend the firm's services. Interestingly the secondary driver of recommendation is ***the support received***. If staff believe they are supported in their role, they believe clients will be appropriately supported and served.

The quality of the work is also the primary driver on the willingness to recommend the firm as a place to work. In this area the secondary driver is ***the opportunity and recognition received***. However ***the quality of the work*** has less impact on staff satisfaction and on loyalty.

When it comes to overall staff satisfaction and commitment to the firm, ***the opportunity and recognition received*** along with ***clarity of the firm's vision*** are the key drivers. Employees want to know that the firm is advancing and so are they. We don't have to have reached the destination yet (e.g. quality of work, market reputation), as long as I can see we are headed in a clear direction.

Staff loyalty however is driven by the two most personal factors. ***The opportunity and recognition received*** and ***the support received***. Where staff believe they are receiving career opportunities, being recognised and supported, they are less likely to indicate a desire to switch firms in the next 12 months.

Key drivers of staff feelings and actions

	Primary Driver	Secondary driver
I feel proud to work for my firm	The quality of the work	
I would recommend the firm's services to clients	The quality of the work	The support received
I would recommend the firm as a place to work	The quality of the work	The opportunity and recognition received
Overall satisfaction	The opportunity and recognition received	Clarity of the firm's vision

I feel committed to my firm	The opportunity and recognition received	Clarity of the firm's vision
I am keen to move firms in the next 12 months	The opportunity and recognition received	The support received

The graduate

Tom was in the final year of his law degree at a leading university. He obtained job offers from a number of leading firms, including his preferred firm, which he believed enjoyed the highest reputation in its market. Let's call them AAA. Given AAA's market leadership, he was somewhat surprised to find that the remuneration they offered was lower than two other firms. Having financially struggled through law school, he decided to raise the issue with AAA as tactfully as he could. Tom called AAA and thanked them for the offer. He went on to say that they may not be aware that their offer was not as competitive as other firms in the market. Tom was surprised by the response. "We know. We're aware that the decision to join our firm is not primarily driven by salary." Tom joined AAA because he recognised the difference in salary was insignificant compared to the opportunity to work with great people, for great clients in a highly regarded firm.

Head-hunting

Gary was approached by a head-hunter to take on a role at an international firm. While the role was similar to the one he currently fulfilled, the firm was larger, provided better opportunities and was willing to pay significantly more. Gary was flattered to be approached for the role. He spoke to a number of contacts who had knowledge of the firm and unfortunately the feedback was far from glowing. While the firm's market reputation was very strong, as an employer they were not highly regarded. Specific concerns were expressed about the way staff were treated in the area Gary would work and how it lacked internal support. Gary discovered that the specific role he was being approached for had been filled by four separate individuals in the last three years. Armed with this information, during an interview Gary asked the firm why they thought they had been unsuccessful in filling this role in recent years. The firm's response to this question - or lack of credible response - confirmed Gary's concerns that he was unlikely to obtain the support or recognition he needed to succeed in the role. Hence, despite the offer of more money and the opportunity to add the firm's brand to his resume, Gary declined the offer.

Retaining the understudy

Sarah was a highly valued manager, working in a niche area within in a medium sized, single office firm. The area she worked in enjoyed a strong market reputation and was highly profitable. While the partner Sarah worked for was the primary face of the offer, Sarah managed the day-to-day relationships with clients and the large team of staff. Unfortunately for Sarah, her supervising partner was unwilling to recommend her for partnership as he did not want to dilute the earnings-per-partner of the practice area. Eventually, Sarah decided to leave the firm to pursue opportunities at another firm. Within 18 months she was made a partner while the practice at her previous firm continues to struggle to perform in her absence.

Firm performance

So having identified what's important to staff, how are firms doing in satisfying them? Firstly, the good news. A testament to the quality of law firms today, 82% of law firm employees were highly likely (8-10 out of 10) to recommend their firm's services to clients. A whopping 53% of respondents responded with a 10 out of 10 to this question. It is not just that they feel they should. It is based on high ratings for each question that formed a part the key driver namely ***the quality of the work*** factor. Every one of these questions rated above 8 out of 10. No other question in the research rated above 7.6. And that's the problem.

The worst performing areas, according to respondents related to ***the opportunity and recognition I receive*** and ***the support I receive*** - the very things that drive satisfaction and loyalty. As a result, a third of law firm employees are keen to move firms in the next 12 months. The financial impact of such dislocation to firms is huge. The loss of revenue, cost of recruitment, cost to develop and integrate new staff and the lost productivity caused as a result represent significant costs to firms.

Summary

While this research focused on the legal profession, we believe the implications are relevant to all professional service firms.

A focus on the quality of work is essential to driving pride in the firm. This, is turn, drives staff recommendations, both to clients and prospective employees. The employer brand in the marketplace will primarily be impacted by this factor.

To improve staff satisfaction, to build commitment and to increase staff retention more is needed. To achieve these outcomes firms need to ensure staff understand the firm's vision and they each receive the opportunity, support and recognition they desire. This has significant implications for:

- Ensuring the firm leadership is visible, open and willing to engage in discussions regarding the direction of the firm
- Ensuring performance management processes are in place and that line managers (usually partners) are active and effective in supporting the processes
- Supporting all staff to do their job effectively including from internal support departments, and
- Monitoring staff satisfaction in these areas to actively manage staff satisfaction, commitment and retention.

With so many staff indicating a desire to move on, the financial impact is too large to ignore. However, if you have a glass half full mentality, a significant opportunity exists for firms to attract new staff - in particular those firms with strong employer brands.

Our focus here has been on what attracts and retains talented people in law firm and in professional services firms more widely. The employer brands of these firms are driven by what people - existing staff and former staff – say about their experience in the firm. In today's world, professionals at all levels are highly networked, with an array of ongoing conversations between them about their working experiences. This is why engagement surveys, continuing real dialogue with people in firms and research of the kind discussed here are critical in evaluating and working on employer reputations, or brands.

Colin Jasper founded Jasper Consulting to assist professional service firms create greater value for their clients and capture a fair share of that value for themselves.

Lisa Hart is CEO of Acritas, a UK-based research house that is the world's leading providers of evidence-based market insights to the legal sector.

Employer branding at Kraft Foods

Peter Brydon and Jenny Gillam

Kraft Foods today

Kraft Foods Inc is the world's second largest food company, making delicious products that people love. The global organisation operates in 170 countries with annual revenues of approximately US$50 billion. Following the global acquisition of Cadbury in 2010, the portfolio features 12 iconic brands including *Kraft, Cadbury, Jacobs, Maxwell House, Trident, Tang, Milka, Nabisco, Oreo* and *Philadelphia.* Many of the brands are recognised the world over, others are favourites in a single country.

- Approximately 70 of Kraft Food's brands have revenues greater than US$100 million
- More than 40 brands are at least 100 years old
- 130,000 employees worldwide work to make delicious food consumers can feel good about
- Kraft Foods makes a difference in the community by fighting hunger and supporting healthy lifestyles

Kraft Foods Australia New Zealand is an integral part of Kraft Foods Asia Pacific and is viewed as a critical talent pipeline for the region. Locally, Kraft Foods Aust/NZ is a company enriched with tradition including more than 100 years of production. Headquartered in Melbourne, Kraft Foods Aust/NZ[1] employs more than 3,500 employees and operates six manufacturing plants. It is regarded as one of the top FMCG businesses with leading brands including Cadbury Dairy Milk, Vegemite, Philadelphia, The Natural Confectionary Company, Cherry Ripe and Oreo.

History

Whether you grew up with Vegemite or Cadbury chocolate, you and your family have probably enjoyed our products which are found in approximately 90 percent of Australian households. In fact Cadbury has been judged as Australia's most trusted brand and Vegemite the most loved.

Although Kraft and Cadbury only came together in 2010, the origin of their strong brand reputations can be traced back more than 100 years ago when two inspiring men from opposite sides of the world, James Kraft and John Cadbury, had a vision to make nutritious and great-tasting snacks that people would love. Hard work and imagination helped grow both organisations into a company that brings more than one billion people their favourite foods every day. Kraft expanded to Australia in 1926 through a partnership with the Fred Walker Cheese Company. Kraft immediately found success, with its cheeses becoming a staple product in most Australian households, closely followed by the Australian icon – Vegemite.

Dissatisfied with the quality of cocoa products, John Cadbury's sons took a momentous step in 1866 that revolutionised the British cocoa business. The brothers began using a cocoa press which produced a more palatable cocoa essence. The marketing of this cocoa essence helped Cadbury to become the successful global brand that it is today. In 1922, Cadbury opened its first overseas factory site in Claremont, Tasmania. From the beginning, both companies were dedicated to looking after their people.

Kraft Foods acquires Cadbury

When Kraft Foods acquired Cadbury in 2010 the integration of two iconic businesses commenced. The history of both organisations and then their merger is the story of brands from six continents coming together as one. As the world's second largest food company, the challenge is to stay nimble, keep it simple and unleash the full potential of the people working in the business. It does this by giving leaders the autonomy to determine the best course of action for their part of the business while still enabling them to benefit from the company's advantage of scale. This gives unique opportunities to build the business and provides people with great development prospects, ensuring Kraft Food's leaders can inspire their teams, act with courage and continuously drive for results.

Having summarised our history and explained something of our corporate brands, we will now turn to a discussion of our employment brand.

Development of an EVP

To attract and retain the best leaders and talent for the business, work is now being done to develop both a global and an Aust/NZ Employee Value Proposition. From the research that has been gathered to date, the things that Kraft Foods Aust/NZ employees report as valuing most are social interactions, achievement and an enjoyable working environment. In addition, the things that they value most highly in an employer are the people of the organization, development of skills, and having interesting and challenging work: in other words, opportunities for career development

The research also found that EVP strengths already existing at Kraft Foods Aust/NZ are:

1. The company has a good brand reputation
2. It is a humanitarian organization (it gives back to society)
3. It is customer and consumer oriented
4. It has supportive and encouraging colleagues
5. It acts as a springboard for future employment

Employees ranked the following areas for Improvement:

1. To provide more fun at work
2. To provide a happier work environment
3. More encouragement so you feel good about yourself as a result of working for Kraft Foods
4. To provide an exciting environment
5. To provide more recognition and appreciation from management

Overall, while many characteristics of Kraft Foods are a good fit with what employees want - such as being an organization which delivers great results - other employee motivations, such as social, fun, and learning are not being fully met by the character of the company today.

Comments on what sets Kraft Foods apart as an employer - the differentiators in Kraft Foods Aust/NZ, included:

- "Very result driven."
- "I love the quality of the brands."
- "The power brands such as Vegemite and Cadbury Dairy Milk provide a sustainable future and career growth."
- "I really enjoy working with the calibre of people that are around you, to a large extent they are driven and focused."

Further work is still to be done in developing both a global EVP and a local EVP, however the intent is to leverage Kraft Foods current performance-focused organizational strengths and to connect with one of the dominant motivations of both employees and candidates - that of personal and career development. Building upon this foundation, our aim is to introduce a more dynamic, entrepreneurial element that captures Kraft Foods drive for innovation, empowerment and growth.

The type of signature experience Kraft Foods Aust/NZ is aiming for upon joining the organisation is that there will be a surprising wealth of opportunities and resources for personal development, learning and advancement. People at every level will be empowered, will be able to create their own destiny and help shape the success of the company.

Kraft Foods Aust/NZ mission for 2011

The Kraft Foods Aust/NZ mission for 2011 supports this vision. As a business Kraft Foods is focused on 'the Three C's':

- "Reigniting the core" by investing in its brands, having strong sales execution and building the innovation pipeline;
- "Achieving a best cost position" by improving supply chain productivity, lifting quality and customer service and reducing overheads; and
- "Building a performance-driven, values led culture" by living the values and putting safety first; elevating people development and embedding systems and processes.

"Fuel 2011" an innovative Development Program

Focusing on the Three C's helped deliver a strong performance for Kraft Foods during the first half of 2011. It was also the platform for launching a number of key initiatives designed to strengthen Kraft Food's employee value proposition. This included a week long development program called Fuel 2011 which was aimed at elevating people development across the business. More than 500 salaried employees across Aust/NZ participated in 13 development programs, a day-long functional expo and a networking evening.

As an Aust/NZ initiative, the program was designed to provide employees with opportunities for development, a chance to learn more about other areas of the business and a platform to build networks with their colleagues. It demonstrated commitment to helping our people develop their broad leadership capability, along with deep functional expertise. The program also enabled cross-functional collaboration to drive business and personal growth.

Fuel 2011 represented a significant turning point in the engagement of our people and we are looking forward to 'Fuel' being enshrined as the highlight of our year-round development program on an ongoing basis. We felt that this initiative met a number of the criteria that Kraft Food's employees told us they were seeking in an employer - social, fun, excitement and learning.

However this is not the only attribute of our workplace we are working on. As mentioned earlier, our research - and most external research around building a strong employment brand - identifies the importance of several attributes in the wider corporate brand. People do value working with an organisation which does good work in the community and which adheres to strong levels of social and environmental responsibility.

With this in mind, other important elements of Kraft Food's brand in the community include:

Kraft Foods is committed to using sustainable supply chains

Kraft Foods takes seriously its responsibility to ensure product materials are sourced from sustainable supply chains. A key public commitment involved Cadbury Dairy Milk chocolate achieving Fairtrade Certification in Australia in 2010.

Kraft Foods is taking steps to reduce its ecological footprint

As a food company, we depend on the Earth's resources every day to make our products. Kraft Foods has made considerable strides to minimise its footprint while continuing to provide quality products to their customers. As part of this:

- Kraft Foods Aust/NZ redeveloped its Vegemite manufacturing process; reducing wastewater by 65 percent and energy consumption by 52 percent (2002 to 2009). Subsequently this initiative was awarded Australia's most prestigious environmental accolade: the **2009 Banksia Environmental Award**.
- At its Ringwood factory, Kraft Foods recently installed rain water harvesting infrastructure which **saves 4 million litres per annum**.

Kraft Foods is committed to enriching the communities in which it operates

Community activities include:

- Kraft Foods Aust/NZ is a major supporter of Foodbank, Australia's leading not-for-profit organisation that distributes food industry donations to the hungry.

- Kraft Foods and the Cadbury brand is the Principal and Strategic Partner of The Humour Foundation which brings joy to the lives of children in hospital through the work of the Clown Doctors.
- Employees are encouraged to volunteer in the community during the annual Delicious Difference Week, as well as in programs throughout the year which are based around CSR three pillars – Education and Enterprise, Health and Wellness, and Environmental Sustainability.

Summary

At Kraft Foods our purpose is simple: make today delicious. Each and every one of our employees has the opportunity to effect change, working with our suppliers, customers and consumers to create a safer, more sustainable and delicious community.

We understand that actions speak louder than words, so at Kraft Foods we give a lot of attention to actions and practices which reinforce these values:

- We inspire trust.
- We act like owners
- We keep it simple
- We are open and inclusive
- We tell it like it is
- We lead from the head and the heart
- We discuss. We decide. We deliver.

We are confident that these values, along with the opportunity to work with amazing brands and inspiring leaders in a global organisation that can offer extensive development opportunities, combine to provide existing and potential employees with an extremely attractive employment proposition.

Peter Brydon
Director Human Resources
Kraft Foods Aust/NZ

Jenny Gillam
Head of Talent Sourcing
Kraft Foods Aust/NZ

[1] We use the acronym "ANZ" here to refer to "Australia and New Zealand". This is not a reference to a bank generally identified with these initials!

Breaking up is hard to do: keeping a strong employment brand after restructure

Hugh Davies and Susan Moir – Macfarlan Lane

One of the most important ways to manifest integrity is to be loyal to those who are not present. In doing so, we build the trust of those who are present. Stephen Covey, 7 Habits of Highly Effective People

In a networked world, trust is the most important currency. Eric Schmidt, University of Pennsylvania Commencement Address, 2009

We think a key driver of an employment brand is in what employees say to others about their real experience at work. Engagement, and an employer brand, is about the emotional connection people have with a company, more than any printed formal statements about what the company stands for. Engagement is built during induction, and then strengthened (or diminished) in the everyday practices, values and behaviours of the organisation's leaders. It is built in and through working relationships, and in the sense people in an organisation have that they are growing, and valued.

Having said this, the time when this reality is at its most poignant is when people are displaced. Culture (and reputation) is formed more during the worst of times than during the best of times. Employment is a psychological "contract" which goes well further than a title, a job description and pay. Restructuring decisions, especially those which see people let go, hit hard at this psychological contract. A brand built carefully over years of individual recruitment and hiring decisions and leadership acts can be tarnished in instant.

Through their work on employee engagement, Hewitt Associates and the Corporate Executive Board found that what matters to people is that organisations deliver on their promises and respect their employees. Current research is increasingly finding a neurological basis for this psychological contract. The human brain is hard-wired to be social. It has evolved to distinguish between "in groups" and "out groups". Evolution provides a strong explanation for this, where exclusion from the group results in vulnerability to predators, starvation and death. We seek to be part of a group of people who are like us. It is rewarding to belong in such a group – we like to see others win if they are like us, and help others out.

Recent neuroimaging work has demonstrated that we feel pain, similar to physical pain, when we experience social rejection or exclusion[2]. In the work context, individuals seek out organisations whose mission and values they can relate to, where the employees they work with are like them, and where they feel they can contribute as part of a group. Acknowledging and acting on the significance of affiliation needs and the impact of disengagement is a real part of managing an ongoing and durable employment brand.

Although corporate loyalty is lower today than it was decades ago, implicit obligations nonetheless remain.

When people are not treated with respect this behaviour will irrefutably damage a company's reputation. The internet enables communication, true or untrue, to be disseminated at the speed of light. We live in an information age. Many stories are shared online about corporate restructures – with an impact on reputations. Here are some examples found and written about in the electronic media:

- More than 2,000 workers at the UK's largest personal injury claims company, The Accident Group (TAG) are coming to terms with redundancy - after many were sacked by text message. Many employees at TAG, which has in the past been accused of aggressive selling methods, spoke of their anger after they learnt of their fate by text message. The message asked recipients to call a number at head office, which contained the voice message from administrators PricewaterhouseCoopers (PwC). It said: "All staff who are being retained will be contacted today. If you have not been spoken to you are therefore being made redundant with immediate effect." A spokeswoman for PwC confirmed that text messages were used in some cases of redundancy, and conceded that the situation was "not ideal"[3].
- The passport service (in the UK) was condemned after boxes of redundancy leaflets were left at the front of its Newport office in full view of staff arriving for work recently. As many as 300 people were facing redundancy. Workers were still in the dark over whether the office would be closed. On closer inspection, the 36 boxes, which were in ripped black bags, had the words "redundancy leaflets" written on them.[4]

- In January 2009, the IBM chief reported strong quarterly profits and in an email addressed to employees stated that, while other companies were cutting back, his would not. "Most importantly, we will invest in our people", he wrote. The next day more than 1,400 employees in IBM's sales and distribution division were told that their jobs would be eliminated in a month. More cuts followed and IBM laid off more than 4,600 North American workers.[5]
- HSBC cut 450 jobs in Asia in 2008. The Hong Kong staff learned that they were losing their jobs in an email from the executive director, Peter Wong. In the email, Mr. Wong said the "exceptionally difficult decision was a result of organizational changes as well as the deteriorating economy. (Chi-fai, Cheuen and Maria Chan: "HSBC to sack 450 in second round of layoffs: HK accounts for bulk of 500 retrenchments in Asia"[6])

As these stories illustrate, social and business networking has made the business community "smaller". People talk with each other much more readily across organisational boundaries and voice their opinions about their experiences. In Australia, there is a substantial network of former staff who have left large iconic firms and who still talk with each other after many years working in other firms. The employment brand of corporates is significantly influenced by what people in these networks say to each other – and they stay connected in their networks for years. Senior people are no different from others in this context: in fact networks amongst senior people across organisations are often quite extensive.

Failure to manage redundancy - or even individual separations - fairly and with clear communication will result in the loss of trust and when trust is gone, it is hard to regain. The discretionary effort from employees, so important in normal times is even more vital with fewer employees doing more work. The employer brand will be damaged and not only will talented employees leave, word of mouth will make it harder to attract the new talent crucial to future company growth. Executives sometimes adopt the attitude that employees fortunate enough to survive should check their emotions at the door and devote their energy to their jobs. In some environments, this is an understandable attitude but it is never justified. Survivors should be the company's best performers, the people it least wants to lose. A study of Fortune 100 companies, in the April 2008 issue of the Academy of Management Journal, showed that it didn't take much downsizing to send the survivors running for the door.

The research sample consisted of employee-friendly companies that were invited to be included in the Fortune magazine "the 100 best companies to work for in America". Layoffs targeting just 1% of the workforce preceded a 31% increase in turnover. The "mere transition from non-downsizer to downsizer" is enough to prompt those who remain to look elsewhere. This is of particular relevance in a sector like financial services, where retention of core skills and experience in times of change is critical in retaining ratings and investment mandates. In this sector, a great deal of significance is placed on performance rewards and short and long term incentives. These things may be needed to create what might be termed base level competitiveness, but they won't build a great employment brand. People who choose to leave often go to work for competitors and the impact is felt years after the restructure.

So how do you retain a strong employment brand when you are poised to restructure (or simply initiate one or two key separations) and as a consequence breach the psychological contract of actual and implied promises made to staff?

Here are five things to think about:

1. Acknowledge to yourselves that you are in fact breaking implied contracts of significance to individuals.

   We isolate ourselves from this reality by saying "this is life" and "people have to live with change". Some firms adopt a transactional, "let's get on with it" demeanour. Restructuring is managed firmly without compassion.

   The most important reality is that each person having to leave is absorbing huge issues internally: issues of self-definition, financial worries, status and the daily affirmation of relationships at work are now being taken away. This truth applies at all levels in a professional hierarchy.

   Recognising all of this is the most important step in retaining a "human" employment brand. Recognition leads to compassion, care and mitigation of the damage otherwise attached to the employment brand of the firm.

2. Make a thoughtful and scrupulously fair process the first and most enduring priority. In each step of the restructuring project, this priority needs to be the first

to be addressed and then exemplified in the behaviours and procedures.

3. Plan a communication process, firstly around conversations with directly affected people and then around how those indirectly affected will be engaged.

   With those directly affected, think about the needs and interests of each individual. Manage each step in the process with compassion and dignity. Work out a tailored approach for each individual – and do it face to face. This is not an event to be delegated.

4. Within the wider community of your organisation, the rules in effectively communicating significant change are
   - communicate face to face and often
   - be honest
   - listen to and engage everyone at an individual level: equip leaders to do this.

   In fact, there is no better process (during restructuring) than being visible and personally engaging with those affected during the implementation of downsizing decisions. Even with those only indirectly affected, this is a time when leaders should not delegate: they should take the lead in personally breaking bad news – face to face, and spending a little time with those involved, being compassionate and thoughtful. This can make a huge impact which will resonate for years in the way employees and ex-employees reflect on the organisation's values and reputation.

   External messages are also important. "We will do everything we can to redeploy rather than retrench, and for those who do have to leave, we will offer extensive support to help them rebuild careers."

5. Ensure that those who must leave are fully supported in rebuilding their careers. Test career transition suppliers: meet the consultants involved to ensure that the support services do deliver a coaching based service where senior people leaving your firm are matched with appropriately senior consultants in open ended, tailored services.

   Don't buy a commoditised service based essentially on price. Look beneath the promises all suppliers make and carefully assess the depth of the service and the seniority of those who will work with your people. Consider surveying those who have left to measure the quality of their experience (a major bank in Australia is now doing this.)

6. Look after the "survivors" as well. Support their disruption and concerns. Explain the support being given to those who have left, engage them also in staying in touch and offering their support to those who must leave. Enrol them in designing the future work of their area.

An employment brand exists in the minds of prospective, current and past employees. We believe that it is what happens in the most testing of times, a restructuring, that can retain and even strengthen an employment brand. What people say to others in these situations creates a more lasting impression than stories offered during recruitment or in everyday practices. Achieving a strong employment brand at times like these rests on taking care of those whose "contract" has been broken. Employees who are retrenched off can and will blog or Twitter about the good or bad experience they endured. The risk of the bad press in this form is lessened to the extent that each separation is handled with compassion and care. If survivors believe their employer is fundamentally reshaping the company for future stability and success while treating people with dignity, they will likely reward the organisation with their best efforts.

Hugh Davies is the Managing Director of Macfarlan Lane and Susan Moir is a Director. Macfarlan Lane is a firm which provides career transition and career development services only for CEOs, and senior executives. The firm operates in most capital cities in Australia, deploying senior consultants who bring significant commercial and leadership experience to each engagement. Their website is www.macfarlanlane.com.au

As something of a post-script, what is Macfarlan Lane's employment brand? What is it that engages those who work in our firm and which leads others to be interested in working with us?

This is what we have distilled in a few conversations amongst us:

> *Macfarlan Lane sets out to build trusted advisor status with the people we work with in the context of career development and career transition.*
>
> *We value collegiality, energy, enthusiasm, respect for confidences, integrity and continuous growth in our insights around coaching and career development.*

Breaking up is hard to do: keeping a strong employment brand after restructure

[2] Eisenberger NI, Lieberman MD, Williams KD. *Does rejection hurt? an fMRI study of social exclusion*. Science 2003; 302:290–2.

[3] http://www.dailymail.co.uk/news/article-182944/Claims-workers-sacked-text-message.html

[4] http://www.southwalesargus.co.uk/news/passport_office/9017198.PASSPORT_OFFICE_Union_fury_over_redundancy_leaflets/

[5] http://www.nytimes.com/2009/03/06/business/06layoffs.html

[6] South China Morning Post 18, November 2008. Web. 05, April 2009.

Transforming BP ANZ's Employment Brand to restore confidence following a catastrophe

Chris Lokum

The catastrophe

On the evening of April 20 2010 a tragic event occurred that had a significant impact on a number of organisations, including BP. A gas release and subsequent explosion occurred on the Deepwater Horizon oil rig which was drilling the Macondo exploration well for BP in the Gulf of Mexico. 11 people died and many others were injured. Hydrocarbons leaked into the water of the Gulf of Mexico for 87 days before the well was closed and sealed.

The initial explosions and subsequent oil leak not only resulted in loss of life and injury, but also impacted the coasts of Louisiana, Mississippi, Alabama, Texas and Florida including the livelihoods of the people living on those coasts. The impacts were widespread and sparked emotional responses across the globe.

In the 2 months following the accident, the BP share price lost 54% of its value and at one point the market capitalisation of the company was down over GBP40bn (cAUD70bn June 2010). In addition, the downgrading of BP's credit rating saw the cost of debt rise swiftly as well as access to debt becoming more difficult, resulting in capital constraints. The accident also drew major political focus with President Obama making a number of visits to the Gulf Coast, in addition, there were calls for BP to face criminal proceedings and the US Senate hearings to ascertain the issues involved – all of which were played out in the glare of the world's media.

What was less visible after the accident was the impact on BP staff and how they and individuals outside of the company altered their view of the company as an employer. The words 'shock' and 'grief' aptly describe the feeling of BP employees. All BP employees carried a reputational burden for the Deepwater Horizon accident and whilst the most intense pressure was felt in the United States, the impact was felt significantly throughout BP's operations in Australia and New Zealand.

Health & Safety sits at the centre of BP's operations in Australia and New Zealand and remains the key priority. Employees began to question whether the Company's priorities and processes were sufficient. For those outside BP, what was once a stable, successful global organisation suddenly looked like a risky option and one that no longer warranted trust and respect.

The response

The immediate impact of the accident and the response over the initial weeks and months was highly visible. At its peak there were over 46,000 people deployed and over 6000 vessels and 110 aircraft mobilised in the response efforts. BP took responsibility for the clean-up, responded swiftly to compensate people affected by the impact of the accident, and implemented a number of steps to protect the health, safety and welfare of the large number of residents and people who helped respond to the accident. Over US$17 billion was spent in 2010 on response activities alone. Throughout, BP sought to work closely with government, local residents, shareholders, employees, the wider industry and the media.

Paul Waterman, President of BP Australia and New Zealand, stated that "the Deepwater Horizon tragedy has cast a shadow over BP and adversely impacted the Gulf of Mexico.

The firm and our people were devastated by the loss of life in the Deepwater Horizon accident and by the impact the event had on the environment and the communities." Paul added "that we should never forget that this was a human tragedy…"

Bob Dudley promised in October 2010 that his top two priorities were making BP the safest oil company in the world and restoring public trust in it. Bob Dudley has said that BP is determined to learn the lessons for the future which arise from the Deepwater Horizon accident and to share them fully throughout the industry. People are at the heart of our progress in BP. Our performance and our safety track record depend on their skill and commitment.

These sentiments set the tone of cultural shifts and organisational changes that would significantly influence the work that was already underway here in Australia and New Zealand to clearly articulate and communicate the differentiated work experience at BP ANZ. We now needed to focus attention on earning back trust and meeting our commitments to restoring economic and environmental damage resulting from the accident. Beyond restoration and building trust, we needed to convince current and potential employees that BP represents an employer brand they should be proud to associate with.

The impact on the employment brand

The scale of the reputational damage to the BP employment brand can be illustrated by the multi-faceted nature of the incident. In BP Australia and New Zealand (BP ANZ) reputational damage was experienced across a number of different perspectives that negatively affect market perceptions of an organisation, as illustrated in the CLC model (See below).

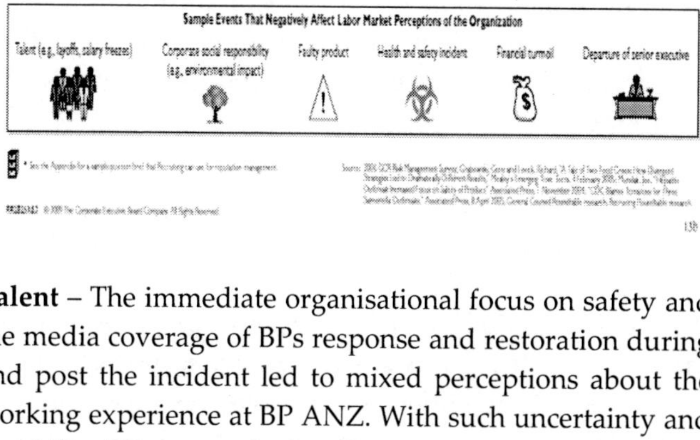

Talent – The immediate organisational focus on safety and the media coverage of BPs response and restoration during and post the incident led to mixed perceptions about the working experience at BP ANZ. With such uncertainty and instability BP was undoubtedly questioned in terms of it's attractiveness in an already tight talent market.

Corporate Social Responsibility – The enormity of the catastrophe attracted intense worldwide media attention and affected BPs reputation in Australia and New Zealand as a 'green and progressive' energy organisation committed to corporate social responsibility. This was crucial as BP was in the process of applying for exploration licenses in South Australia.

Health and safety incident – The loss of life and serious injury damaged the previously strong reputation for sustainable safe operations that BP ANZ stood for.

Financial turmoil – Plunges in the share price and market capitalisation indicated a loss of confidence in BP throughout the external market and serious questioning over the long-term financial stability and viability. This is a key attraction attribute where confidence needed to be restored quickly.

Departure of senior executives – On 27 July 2010, BP confirmed that CEO Tony Hayward would resign and be replaced by Bob Dudley on 1 October 2010. Although the transition was seamless, this leadership change and others that occurred with it created a period of uncertainty for some employees.

Building the Employee Value Proposition

Whilst recognition of the criticality of focus on our Employment Brand was already on the agenda as a result of increased competition in the resources sector and the tight talent market existing in Australia and New Zealand, the Deepwater Horizon accident had a significant impact on the direction and implementation of the proposition at that point in time.

BP ANZ began the EVP journey in March 2009 at which point it was recognised that a strong employment brand would be essential to the long term survival of the organisation. Without strong talent who are engaged, we cannot deliver our business priorities.

Our initial focus was to develop the BP ANZ Employee Value Proposition (EVP) that would ultimately underpin an employment branding strategy. A compelling EVP would provide a measure of the balance between what an employee receives from BP in return for their performance on the job. That is, it is the 'get' versus the 'give'. If in the employees' minds they 'get' rewards equal to or exceeding what they 'give', a company will tend to have more satisfied employees and increased retention.

What the employee 'gets' is not just about tangible 'rewards' – intangible elements such as values and culture are also powerful drivers of employee engagement. A belief that 'what matters to me, matters to the company' promotes alignment to company strategy and performance and encourages a stronger sense of advocacy.

A compelling proposition leads to a competitive and differentiated employment brand

After building and communicating the EVP internally, the next phase was to leverage this proposition in terms of an employment brand. Furthermore, an employment brand is important to increasing employee engagement, which correlates with satisfaction, productivity and performance.

BP's Employment Brand is intrinsically linked to the Corporate Brand. Strong alignment between the two Brands ensures consistency of messaging. Where there is incongruity between the Employment and Corporate Brands, it can create confusion. Messages and priorities can be conflicting and priorities become unclear. For that reason, we needed to ensure that the EVP and Employment Branding accurately represented the working environment and cultural shifts post the incident.

Figure 1 illustrates how the Corporate Brand and the Employment Brand and the EVP are inextricably linked.

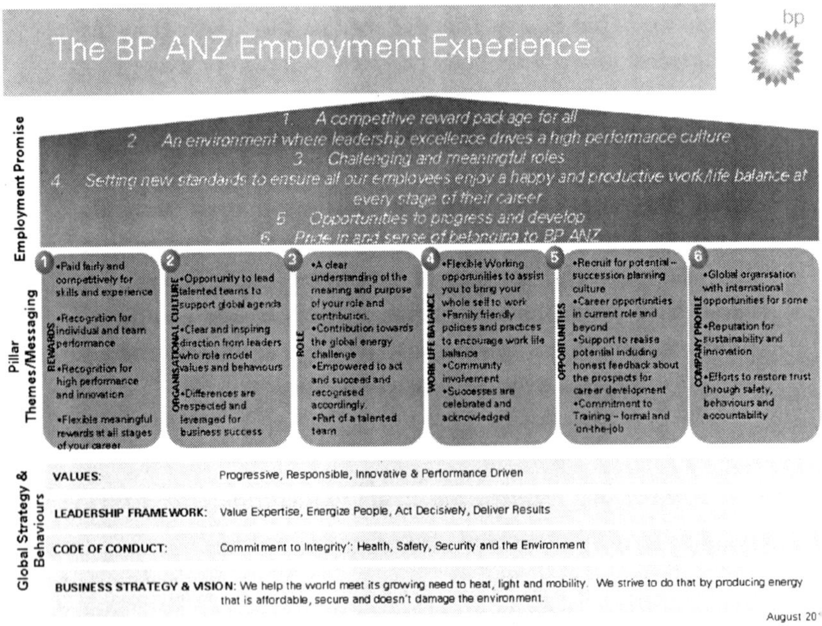

So how does BP begin to restore its reputation?

In April 2010 at the time of the accident, we had built and were continuing to internally communicate a strong proposition around the 'Rewards', 'Work/Life Balance' and 'Culture – Leadership' pillars. We knew after the accident that we needed to quickly change our priorities to focusing on safety, stability, maintaining operational performance, health & resilience and above all rebuilding trust.

Safety

The first priority following the Deepwater Horizon accident was safety. Employees needed to understand that their safety and that of our entire business remained our No1 priority. Visible steps were taken to review the risks to the business and ensure compliance with BP's enhanced safety standards.

Once the well was capped, BP took a number of steps to change organisation structures in the Exploration and Production business to provide greater clarity and accountability as well as bringing specialists together into teams where they can build their capability. The organisational changes also included the creation of an enhanced safety and risk function with increased powers and independence to drive consistent and improved safety focus across BP operations and the development of a globally consistent Performance Management system which has safety, operational rigour and clear group values and behaviours at its heart. Safety improvements are already, "rippling through the company," according to Mark Bly, the head of BP's new safety organization.

We recognise that providing energy safely and reliably is essential for our future business success in Australia and New Zealand. Our goal remains to operate with "no accidents, no harm to people and no damage to the environment". We are working with renewed effort to achieve this aim.

Stability

The next priority was to stabilise the workforce and this effort continued well after the leak was stopped. Our research showed that companies which underestimate the importance of effective employee engagement during such a time often suffer significant economic damage as a result of, among other reasons, a lack of trust, low morale, a loss of focus and potentially the loss of well trained and dedicated employees. This in turn, also lengthens the timeline it takes for the company to emerge from the crisis.

Recovery and restoration efforts along with the progress we have made to date reinforce to our employees and the market that we are still a financially strong organisation following events in the Gulf of Mexico.

Maintaining momentum

Maintaining business momentum also became a strong focus for the organisation. This was heavily dependent upon each employee feeling confident that the Company would resolve the problems it faced and therefore they would choose to deliver their extra discretionary effort. Leadership style, commitment and authenticity were seen as the key enablers.

Leaders across the BP ANZ businesses were encouraged to be present, be visible and be there for their team. They needed to do their homework and be clear about what was known about the Deepwater Horizon accident. Employees needed a safe space to discuss their feelings, fears and concerns. Leaders were encouraged to openly discuss the situation in team meetings (face-to-face wherever possible) and to spend at least 20% of their week holding individual discussions and team meetings, listening to concerns and fears, answering questions and helping people remain focused on team goals and deliverables and reiterating the need to continue focusing on safety and operations. Providing factual information was essential to dispel the hype caused by the media and leaders were advised not to speculate. Senior leaders from the BP Group provided regular update meetings and locally, leaders cascaded this information to employees.

BP established a $20 billion trust fund to meet individual, business and government claims, as well as the cost of the Natural Resource Damages. The physical rebuilding was in many ways seen as a 'United States' issue but the emotional impact and the damage to the trust in BP and our reputation in the market was felt as keenly in Australia and New Zealand as in other regions. The worldwide public interest in the accident meant that it was impossible to segregate the geography where the accident had taken place from the rest of the organisation, but even had this been possible there was no desire from BP to step away from global corporate responsibility or the company wide learning and view this simply as a US issue.

Health and resilience

Employees across Australia and New Zealand were encouraged to take their annual leave and they were encouraged to watch out for each other. Use of the Employee Assistance Programme, which provides confidential counselling and support to staff members and their families, was actively promoted.

Trust

The primary focus in BP ANZ has been on rebuilding trust with employees and key external stakeholder groups and rebuilding employee advocacy for what we offer and stand for. Significant work has gone into engaging employees in the breadth of our employment proposition to help them understand what BP is able to provide in recognition of their continued commitment and performance. It has been a deliberate strategy to re-engage internally and build employee advocacy before actively promoting our employee value proposition externally through employment branding.

The process of rebuilding the BP employer brand in ANZ is a journey. The trust that took an instant to lose will take considerable time to bring back up to the levels we expect, but significant progress is being made. What we have learnt is a number of critical lessons:

- Live up to our commitments to respond to the accident, pay legitimate claims and embed the learnings from the accident across BP's business worldwide.
- Authenticity is critical – employees must feel as well as hear the message and believe their leader genuinely cares about their concerns.
- Our offer must be compelling but simply articulated – never is this more important than when everyone is questioning your organisation and what it stands for.
- The messaging must be consistent and reinforced with tangible actions, erring on the side of disclosure and transparency.
- We must constantly measure and sense check the perceptions of our existing employees and those we value in the market and adapt our proposition to remain compelling and authentic.

Chris Lokum is the HR Director for BP Australia and New Zealand. This organisation, as a part of the wider

multinational BP Group, is engaged in the exploration for and production of oil, natural gas and liquefied natural gas and the refining, transportation and marketing of petroleum and lubricant products, as well as power trading and marketing of solar photovoltaic products. The business has 10,000 employees.

<u>Bibliography</u>

- The Employee Value proposition: 6 Things You Need to Know, Davis Advertising
- The Speed of Trust, Stephen Covey with Rebecca Merrill, 2006, Simon & Schuster Inc
- Corporate Leadership Council, Reputation for Recruiting, 2006

Brand first, recruit second – what happens to your employer brand when you engage an intermediary?

Jim Bailey – Bailey, Shaw

What is a brand? Simply a person's gut feel for a product, service, or organisation. Many companies spend millions on their corporate brand identity. But they spend a lot less on defining an employment brand. Indeed some companies assume, perhaps arrogantly, that their corporate brand is enough to attract people to work for them.

Take a look at your employment brand. Can you define it? Imagine going into a supermarket, seeing lots of product on the shelves, but all of it looks the same and is in white packaging. Would your company allow its product/service offering to be so bland and not stand out? So why allow the employment brand to be that white, blank packaging that is not unique and stand out? Or have it stand out for the wrong reasons.

Employment brand is a vast subject and we will just touch here on how some key messages can impact the process of recruiting talent into an organisation. Key messages which can be easily enhanced....or diluted. The best and most effective employer brand strategy is truly mirrored within an organisation in how all employees are treated. It has its key values and messages delivered upon and communicated at every opportunity.

People are naturally social. They love to talk. Gossip. They are hungry for information. When looking at employment branding, people want relationships with people, not faceless, bureaucratic organisations. So the key is allowing people to have transparent, trustworthy, two-way communication with your organisation, whether you engage them directly or you turn to another party to do it for you.

First, a quick run through the world of recruitment for those not familiar with its modes of operating. Naturally each organisation is different, and also approaches the attraction of candidates using a varying mix of media and resources. However we find that the worlds of senior executives and other employees are quite different.

By Senior Executives, we count those who make up the board, report direct to the board (CEO and equivalent) and who report on a level one below that. Typically these attraction assignments are completed through Executive Search, using external agencies. Their services usually include benchmarking candidates against the external world or identified internal employees.

When it comes to the broader base of employees spanning upper to middle management, technical specialists and operational and support employees, a variety of methods are used to identify, attract and evaluate potential talent. These include, but are certainly not limited to:

- Search (typically using external resources)

- Selection (using both external and internal resourcing activities). In recent years, the growth and use of employee databases has increased and will continue to do so, due to advances in technology.
- Word of mouth, which can be from internal referral programs, a range of social media, and/or direct contact with those personally known or made known through sources.

Engaging an external consultancy

There are some inbuilt pitfalls in the recruitment processes. When you engage an external consultant to complete a search, there is an inbuilt tension between the promotion of the client's employer branding and that of the search organisation. Opportunities to build positive associations…..and to create potential disconnects.

In our experience, potential candidates when approached by an external person acting for the employer will first make judgements and reactions to the person approaching them. During the "wooing phase" they will reflect on how they are dealt with during that part of the process as indicative of how the organisation might deal with them. So in assessing recruitment and talent attraction suppliers, organisations need to ensure informed associations are built and that they are confident the approach part of the process is done 'professionally and well' and the follow up stage also impresses the candidate.

Areas to attend to here in assessing the supplier are:

- Tone and manner (mutual respect) from the initial contact onwards,

- The format and accuracy of information provided,
- Communication regularity, frequency and content from the consulting organisation,
- Rigour (and relevance) of the process itself,
- Time taken to work through a process and make a decision, by both the consulting organisation and the client in question.

Once the potential candidate becomes interested and is qualified as a contender, and the ultimate organisation's identity is revealed, then the employer branding of the hiring organisation will come into play.

Whatever the recruitment firm and the ultimate organisation may have said about themselves, the candidate will typically start from the point of either knowing or not knowing something of the organisation's 'reputation'.

They will reach this point of view based upon a wide variety of factors, which could include things as mundane as the next door neighbour's personal point of view, having had a bad (or good) experience with a particular organisation, or having seen a media advertisement from the organisation which the candidate views as having been very clever and to the point.

Whenever we work with 'good' organisations, it is easier. At the briefing stage, it's clear that a number of issues likely to be important to the talent being sought have been thought through, and delivered upon. The key element is track record. If the topic is promotion prospects, what has been the history of moving up and out of this job? With training – what's on offer to people in this role? If it's intellectual challenge – what does the organisation typically demand of people in this role, and how do they support their development through 'extra' challenges? And so on.

So, when you brief a recruitment firm (or an internal person) to find you somebody, what thoughts should you give to employer branding?

Make sure you retain control

Are you abdicating or delegating? Given the clamour for your time in today's busy business world, it is all too easy to assume that the consultant you have selected to represent your firm understands the key messages which are vital to setting candidate expectations correctly about your organisation. Make sure they grasp and are able to articulate the essence of your employer brand.

If written materials are to be presented on your behalf, then they should be thorough, accurate, professional, and contain those key messages.

Whose brand is being represented?

An obvious tension exists between recruitment organisations which advertise positions on your behalf using their own branding, versus recruitment organisations which advertise with your branding. In the first case, despite what they may say, using advertising over their logo distributes and enhances their brand, as well as increasing their stockpile of potential candidates, for your and other client positions.

Where they use your brand, consider whether the messages which come across are those which you would want people to receive, who are coming in contact with your organisation through an intermediary?

Representing remuneration

Consider the potentially contentious aspect of advertising remuneration. Typically, in our experience, where an organisation either advertises over its own brand itself, or insists that we do so, remuneration is usually not specifically included.

Our advice is consistent in that regard, in that advertising for any position without including indicative remuneration is not to be recommended. We have all had the experience of looking at a house advertisement, or a motor vehicle advertisement, or a fashion advertisement, which does not include the pricing and not being able to make a decision. Most of the time, we move on without responding.

The rationale by most organisations is that they would rather not advertise the remuneration, because it makes it public and all their employees will know. Our contention is that if the organisation is a healthy one, then everyone should know what people are being paid for each position, as such information will typically be known informally, and it should be highly defensible by the host organisation in any case.

Where advertisements do not include the identity of the ultimate organisation, then they quite often include remuneration. This is much more satisfactory for potential candidates and also in relation to the particular position being advertised. However, watch for the possibility that many consulting organisations these days are looking to add to their databases as many people as they can.

The impact of simple courtesy on your employer brand

It is difficult to talk about how employer brands can be shaped without mentioning what we regard as an unfortunately relatively common simple lack of courtesy within the selection arena. Repeatedly in surveys, potential candidates express their annoyance at not receiving anything at all back by way of communication, when they have expressed an interest in a particular role.

Where potential candidates apply for a position, whether that is direct to the ultimate organisation or through an intermediary, it is very easy and low cost these days to acknowledge receipt of such an expression of interest and to subsequently, send a polite, professional decline advice, if this indeed is how the exercise is turning out.

Just think for a minute, how this simple business courtesy can and does influence the employer branding involved in this part of the process.

The influence of word of mouth on employer brand

Since surveys typically report that somewhere around 75% to 90% of appointments to positions are ultimately made by using other than search and selection consultants, then the whole area of word of mouth, at any level, merits further investigation. Word of mouth, or 'the hidden market', can and does yield great success for both candidates and organisations.

For instance, organisations which recognise that people who have left the organisation often form a "communication alumni" can be potentially ahead of the game. Many people return to organisations they used to work for, particularly if they feel they have a lingering connection with them and a reason for doing so. Whoever said that people join organisations and depart because of managers, certainly described something which rings true. In our experience individuals who contact previous direct reports and ask them to join them have a high level of success.

The use of social media is burgeoning too. It is also providing an opportunity for people, whether they work within particular organisations or not, to very quickly communicate their views on what has just happened in their workplace, or what is about to happen. This can dramatically affect the overall representations and the employer branding of organisations.

Everyone is talking about your organisation, whether your executive leadership like it or not. Be it your products, services or leaders ... and, yes, even your organisation as a place to work. Google today: "Working for *****" (insert your employer's name). You can see what people are saying on blogs, websites, and Twitter feeds. Log into Glassdoor.com. Those conversations are taking place right now, (sadly few are taking place on official employer channels/sites, as many don't allow or are closed to any form of engagement or comments).

People love to talk. The difference now is that they tell their friends about their views via mass communication channels and their friends are now large communities. Word of mouth spreads like wildfire. This can be pretty scary for modern organisations as business can no longer control what is said. Recruiters need to embrace this, as much as should your internal PR & Marketing departments.

Assess your structured interview process

The assessment and offer stages of the hiring process provide organisations with an opportunity to engage in two-way communications and build a thorough perception about what life will be like in the organisation for those who join. Managing this perception is critical, as a failure to deliver might not only result in short-term turnover; it could result in talent leaving the organisation disgruntled and happy to talk about it.

Examine your interview process and determine how authentic your efforts are.

Realistic preview

Do the interviewers provide a realistic job preview of both the positive and potentially negative aspects of the organisation, the work culture, and the job?

Opportunity to ask questions

Does your interview structure allocate at least 25% of the time to be spent with a candidate exploring topics of interest to them, i.e. responding to their questions and concerns?

Opportunities to meet others (including peers)

Are interviewees for professional and managerial jobs asked "who they wish to talk to" by title in order to make their job-acceptance decision, and then provided an opportunity to do so?

Review performance expectations

Is time allocated to explain how your company measures job performance and to provide a detailed overview of near-term and long-term performance expectations?

Final Thoughts

Accepting a new job is such an important decision, one that many candidates quite rightly consider life altering. Serving up generic information and failing to invest in being both differentiated and real can render your organisation unattractive in today's connected society. Recruiting organisations (and also internal recruiters) need to be much more adept at thinking about how best to represent employer brand and communicate in an authentic way.

Jim Bailey
Partner

Bailey, Shaw recruits across a range of occupations at senior levels, working down from CEO/MD/GM. The firm specialises in gaining recruitment results, rather than just in specific position categories or industries. Our objective is simple... "To be recognised as the best quality executive recruitment consulting firm in the markets in which we choose to operate"

Building an employer brand to give you a competitive edge

By Tim Grogan

Global forces impacting the labour supply and the pressing challenges of growth in a highly competitive environment mean that talent management has never been more important than it is today. Technological change, an ageing population and acute skill shortages across numerous industries are all creating a sharp focus on managing talent at senior levels in many organisations.

Senior executives look to the human resources function to come up with innovative approaches to attracting, hiring and retaining quality people. Many organisations are becoming more mobile and flexible in their approaches to structuring roles and how work is undertaken. Yet despite these developments, some organisations still don't have a clear concept of how to effectively manage their talent needs. Hiring professionals will inform you what is required to develop a human capital advantage. Getting the business to understand the investment required to achieve it is another story.

The message we have for our clients is that leading edge recruitment and retention are connected by an employer brand. This brand or employment identity is an important part of achieving competitive advantage in the labour market. In some companies recruitment is seen as a transactional based function often based around a shared service model. In more progressive companies recruitment is regarded quite differently. It is more of a sales and marketing function established to help successful organisations be more competitive in their pursuit to attract and retain the brightest talent.

Creating your Employer Brand

So how do these leading edge companies develop an employer brand that helps them build a competitive edge? From our conversations with our clients we have distilled an approach consisting of four steps - Assessment, Strategy, Implement and Measure.

Assessment

To best understand the perceptions of the brand, we speak with the employees to ascertain what matters to them when they assess an organisation and how well it will fit with their career plans. We refer to this assessment process as building the brand from the inside out. The process starts with approaching your people and using focus groups, interviews or a research survey. Participants should include current employees, past employees and a sampling of outside professionals in the organisation's employment market. It is critical to get a cross section of your workforce not just senior management.

Top managers may be somewhat insulated and there can be tendency to overstate the organisation's employment attributes. We have encountered instances where executives believe they do not need to undertake research to develop a brand because they believe they can rely on their own knowledge of the organisation. This confidence should be treated with caution as usually in our experience the research outcomes are quite different. Speaking with your workforce and hearing their first hand experience provides invaluable insights. Using a third party to manage the process usually means people speak more openly about their experiences.

In additional to hearing these internal perspectives it is important to scan the external market to truly understand your competitors' employment attributes. An external scan makes sure you specifically focus on the labour segments you actually compete in, regardless of industry. Today with more people using social media sites such as LinkedIn it's a lot easier to find out about the competition. Recently Dell in the US used Linkedin to review its employer brand using their research insight tools. Linkedin has a solution that enables any organisation to specifically target competitor employees and invite them to participate in an online survey. The tool enabled Dell to rank itself against other organisations and identify the negative perceptions of its employer brand. Equally important is to understand how competitors position themselves in attracting talent to ensure your message will stand out in a crowded market.

Once the research is completed, the information becomes the basis for an analysis that leads to decisions on how to best position your brand. A number of techniques can be employed at this stage. One of the most effective steps when analysing your research is to group the key attributes people have identified into themes. By grouping the data you can create themes that enable you to see the common factors that unite an organisation across division and labour segments. Once you have this in view you are able to then consider the competitive landscape and identify which attributes differentiate you from your competitors.

Employer branding is evolving to bring the relationship between HR and marketing closer together. Over the last 5 years in the Australian market we have seen marketing working closely with HR to drive brand communications. The employer brand is owned by the business, facilitated by marketing and driven by HR. The assessment phase enables HR to educate the business about the employee's voice and create a vision that will ensure they can effectively attract and retain the right people to achieve their business objectives.

Strategy

On completion of the research, developing the employee value proposition (EVP) begins. The EVP represents the detail of the employer brand, the many facets of the value that people recognise in working for an organisation. The EVP looks to summarise the tangible and intangible attributes, the collective experience and perceptions of the brand.

In every organisation people are communicating their perception of the employment experience based on their personal experiences and career aspirations. By defining an EVP we are creating a platform for the organisation to begin to articulate their story through their people in a consistent way. The EVP looks to summarise the tangible and intangible attributes, the collective experience and perceptions of the brand. In a lot of instances organisations like to make their EVP aspirational. Whilst every brand should have an element of aspiration, it's critical that the

EVP is grounded in reality. When employees join an organisation you are instantly assessed on your ability to deliver on your employee promise. If an organisation has developed an EVP that reflects the company they want to be not the company they are today, you may find it to contributing factor to high turnover.

When writing an EVP statement, it is important to use simple language and to clearly articulate the proposition from an employee perspective. The ideal length of an EVP is 50 - 100 words. Like any good story we want to be able to articulate the proposition in a way that is engaging. The proposition should be used as a foundation for all communications. It should complement your internal people strategy and link back to the brand essence of your consumer brand.

Once defined an Employer Brand Theme is developed which summarise your EVP personality, this is often referred to as a tag line. The notion of a tagline which sits on all Employer brand communications creates some challenges from a marketing perspective. Ultimately, it comes down to the organisation, in some instances the tagline stands out on its own, like a sign off reinforcing the proposition at all levels. In other instances the tagline can be integrated into the body copy of the advertisement and the consumer brand tagline is used for brand consistency.

Great examples of Employer brand taglines are GSK "Together we make life better" or Telstra "Connect with what you love". Both these examples sit across all employer brand communications and position the EVP perfectly. Whereas when St George bank launched their employer brand in 2007 with "Succeed in Great", it was only used within the advertisement body copy and the corporate tagline of "Good with people, Good with money" was used as their sign off.

Once a firm defines the brand position it wishes to occupy, it needs to address the creative side and practicalities. The company must create a visual identity that brings the EVP to life and think about how to effectively communicate the message to its target audience. The creative process is critical to the success of the brand. Advertising is a battle of perceptions. The art is to create a combined direction that enables the internal audience to identify within the company and to create something that is unique enough to successfully position it in the external market. It is at this point where the competitor research is invaluable. The external perceptions of your employer reputation enable the creative team to develop a brand identity that respects your corporate guidelines but encapsulates the brand essence of your proposition.

For some organisations, the conservative nature of the corporate brand guidelines can tend to water down the employer brand. This outcome can negate the external opportunities to be competitive and differentiate the organisation from its competitors for talent. When developing your creative message, those who are able to respect the corporate brand guidelines but develop a unique creative message will be best positioned to capture the attention of your target audience.

Pepsi recently made quite an impression when they launched their employer brand "The Power of Possibilities". They built on their strong knowledge as to how to interact with customers. Pepsi took a very customer focused approach on their Careers Site where job-seekers could download options for Pepsi's mobile jobs applications. Knowing the importance of building an emotional connection they used social media to engage the passive candidate market not just use the medium to list job vacancies. PepsiCo's careers Twitter profile has over 4,700 followers and continues the "Possibilities" branding. It is LinkedIn where PepsiCo really stands out. The Careers tab is branded with the "Possibilities" logo, featuring EVP videos and full job listings.

One reminder is that wherever your creative journey takes you, the most important part of the process is achieve approval from your leadership team. It is critical that you are able to present the research findings used to develop the EVP and Employer brand creative. This becomes a powerful way to manage expectations and educate senior management around employer brand.

Implementation

When launching an employer brand, there should be two distinct communication strategies - internal and external. This is where a lot of companies fall down. Few companies are able to articulate how they have implemented their employer brands apart from some recruitment templates on Seek.

When planning how to implement your employer brand, the first step is to outline a plan. Since the employer brand has been built from the inside out, it is always recommended to launch it internally first. After all, it's the employees' brand.

The first step is to audit the internal communications activities that influence the recruitment process (pre and post interview packages, candidate offer/rejection letters, onboarding package, benefits brochure, employee referral or recognition programmes) and other corporate internal communication materials (management presentations, intranet).

Once this is completed partner with your internal communications team to imbed this message within the organisation. It is also important to consider how you want to launch the brand internally so that every employee understands the new brand positioning. When St George first launched their Employer Brand in 2007 Gail Kelly was sending out weekly emails about the performance of the bank. To launch the brand effectively an animated video was created when Gail engaged the iconic dragon in a light hearted discussion about the bank, the importance of their people and the significance of the employer brand message.

Externally the focus is on how the brand is communicated along the Talent Pathway™ from an awareness, attraction and recruitment of the right candidates. Part of the philosophy of developing an employer brand is to proactively communicate your message to influence the labour segments you want to recruit. The objective is to move away from reactive recruitment practices by proactively promoting your employer brand message to build a talent pool of passive candidates.

Matthew Jeffery and Amy McKee believe that only 10% of the talent market are active job seekers. The art of employer branding is to capture the attention of the 90% by inviting them to connect with your brand for future opportunities. Consider your workforce plan and business objectives when you create your annual Talent Sourcing

Strategy including media (print and online), profile sources (CV mining, social networking), recruiting tools (web, email or print collateral) and response management tools (applicant tracking system). A detailed communication plan should be presented to the leadership team for sign off and budget approval. This is the art of employer branding.

Implementation is often the stage where processes can fall short, as organisations fail to deliver the time, effort and resources required to fully implement their well-conceived plans. So many employer brand projects focus on developing an EVP but often the stakeholders end up never getting the necessary support to bring it to life. To have an employer brand is one thing, to activate that brand in a way that influences peoples' perceptions of your workforce, is another.

Recently Telstra launched a graduate campaign with the view to change the way graduates saw them as an employer. The research showed that graduates currently working at Telstra felt that they were selling themselves short and that students on campus didn't fully understand the career opportunity of the organisations. The opportunity was to bring the employer brand to life in a way that would meet this goal. Option City was born and it has been one of the most successful graduate recruitment campaigns ever, www.optioncity.com.au. The quality of candidates and the acceptance of offers are well above best practice.

Measurement

So what is the return on investing in employer branding activities? One way to approach this question is to look at the accuracy of how the brand is understood by important constituencies and audiences. This accuracy is termed "brand strength".

If the employer brand is 100% understood and appreciated by all audiences, it has very high brand strength. In this case, the aim should be to sustain clarity and keep the brand current with organisational change in the context of a dynamic, competitive talent marketplace.

If the employer brand is less than 100% understood and appreciated by all audiences, then the solution is to create greater clarity. The goal should be to strengthen the brand by changing perceptions and bringing them as close as possible to perfect understanding—all the while striving to be 100% current.

When it comes to employer brand strength, a 100% level of understanding or appreciation is purely theoretical. While it may not be attainable, thinking about a perfect score helps frame the improvement needed.

Organisations use a range of tools to measure how employer brand is perceived and understood by various constituencies. These include large scale benchmarking surveys, targeted new hire surveys and other assessment tools linked to employee engagement.

Conclusion

Many organisations lack a holistic view as to what are the real costs of turnover and reactive recruitment practices. Human resources professionals can play a significant role by educating line management around the importance of the talent management process. By clarifying how an integrated approach can impact the bottom line in terms of cost versus benefit, HR can generate support among key leaders.

Companies must strive to live their brands. This is no easy task. It requires organisational and cultural change and sustained commitment …and for the long haul.

Tim Grogan

Tim Grogan – Former Head of Employer Branding, Adcorp, a full service advertising agency specialising in strategic employment communications.
www.adcorp.com.au

Tim's key responsibilities involved Employer Brand development, which he delivered for government and private enterprise clients for over 5 years with Adcorp. Tim's strengths lie in his ability to formulate commercially successful outcomes for clients, whilst strategically contributing to creative brand success.

Tim has worked with clients including Telstra, PwC, WorkSafe Victoria, Oxiana, The Federal Group, ANZ Bank (Asia Pacific), Coles and YMCA in Employer Brand development and deployment.
Twitter: @tgrogan

LinkedIn: au.linkedin.com/in/timgrogan

Insights into the Building of an Employer Brand at Telstra

Brie Macklin

Telstra is one of the iconic Australians. We've been around since the start of last century, and are part of the fabric of the society in which we operate. Through our products and services, we improve the lives of people; in their communities, in business and with their families.

Today we are Australia's largest telecommunications and information services company. We offer a full range of services and compete in all telecommunications markets throughout Australia, providing more than 8.3 million Australian fixed line and 12.2 million mobile services. With more than 35,000 employees, our people live and work in virtually every local community in the country keeping Australia connected.

Many organisations have come to the realisation that an employee value proposition and an employment brand is not just nice to have, but vital to the success of the organisation's ability to attract and retain talent. Having an employment brand, needs to be more than just a tagline, and attractive photography across a careers website and job advertising templates. Today, a brand and employee value proposition needs to mature and evolve in order to remain effective.

Redefining our organization

Now is a very exciting time at Telstra; the world around us is changing and our customers are telling us we must change. We are changing into a sales, services and marketing led company, underpinned by engineering excellence. We recognise every employee plays a role in delivering an improved customer service and contributing to Telstra's ongoing success. Our employment brand is more important now than ever before.

Building an engaged workforce is a key strategic objective for our business. Not only is it built into our shared business goals, we understand when people are engaged and supported at work they are more able to deliver an outstanding customer experience. We are committed to making Telstra a truly great place to work – a culture where employees understand the company strategy and how they contribute to it; where they are supported to do their best and deliver to the strategy; where we encourage employees to work together, collaborating to deliver improvements across the company; and are recognised and rewarded for their efforts.

One of our biggest strengths is that every Australian knows who we are, so inevitably Telstra has a strong existing employment brand. We found this strength did bring with it some challenges. When you touch more Australians than any other company, experiences can vary and we found there were opportunities for improvement to ensure customers, communities and potential employees all viewed Telstra in a consistently positive way.

This was our challenge – to ensure individuals continue to think of Telstra as a company with a strong employment brand, in a constantly evolving industry.

Recruitment challenges ahead

Whilst our organisation is addressing many challenges related to customers, technology and competition, those of us in HR are facing challenges of our own in the quest for talent.

It is predicted there will be a shortage of 19,000 IT professionals in Australia in 2015, and more than 25,000 by 2020. There are more than 20,000 IT jobs advertised on Seek right now. Salaries are being driven up, and organisations are struggling to hire permanent employees and retain the IP in their organisations. We continue to focus on improving our reputation as a preferred employer in this space, where we compete with companies with a more established employer brand - particularly with younger generations.

In an age where innovation, entrepreneurship and individualism are flourishing, many people are no longer as attracted to the benefits of working for a large organisation. We are finding job security, employee benefits and long-term career progression isn't at the top of everyone's career wish lists. It is also quite commonplace for individuals to actively look for other opportunities by joining alternative employers - in both large and smaller organisations - with poaching not unusual in a dynamic industry.

Faced with these challenges, Telstra began implementing a range of initiatives to improve our employment brand.

Taking back ownership

Before 2007, Telstra outsourced its recruitment process to agencies. There was no panel of vendors in place, and we didn't have a careers website. Our employment brand, the messages being communicated, and the profiles of the people we were bringing into our organisation were being determined by our external partners, and not us. We recognised this was the first change we needed to make.

To deliver on our business strategy we clearly needed to attract and retain the best people in the market place, with the right skills and capabilities. In order to do this, a number of further changes needed to be made. The Telstra Careers Centre was formed utilising a recruitment process outsourcing (RPO) model, and bit by bit we've brought all of our recruitment back in-house. We also understood by defining our employee value proposition and developing the employment brand to communicate it, we would improve our attractiveness and our ability to source from a much deeper pool of talent in the labour market, increase the commitment levels of our employees and, over time, would reduce the compensation required to bring in new talent.

Rebuilding our employee value proposition and employment brand

Before embarking on a brand development activity it was extremely important for us to conduct external research on our employment brand perceptions. In 2007 we ran an external survey of 1000 participants and held a number of focus groups with participants that were reflective of the types of employees we have in our workforce.

The findings of this research were somewhat expected considering our history… as well as enlightening in part. Some general perceptions about Telstra included:

"Large and monolithic"
"Inefficient, conservative and inflexible"
"Not progressive"
"Impersonal, exploitative, a cube city"
"Limited, boring career opportunities"

The biggest outtake for us was the perception that career options were limited at Telstra. Most people believed that we only offered jobs in a call centre or as a technician in the field. We were also viewed as having a heavily male dominated and aging workforce.

Looking internally through qualitative and quantitative research methods with representatives across our organisation, we then explored the profile of successful people at Telstra; what qualities, behaviours and attitudes had been necessary for them to succeed in a career here. We uncovered what was important to our people in their careers and to what extent they were experiencing those attributes during their time at Telstra. We identified in detail what our employee value proposition was, and we then gave some hard thought on how best to deliver this message more widely.

The objectives for our employment brand were quite simple. We wanted people to think Telstra is a great place to work; that Telstra looks after its employees by offering real career development opportunities, recognising high performance and providing a supportive and flexible working environment – with flexibility options to suit individual needs. We wanted people to feel they would be happy and fulfilled working at Telstra and proud to say they were a member of the team at Telstra. We wanted people to act on this by visiting our careers website and applying for one or many of our roles.

The creative development process was a tricky one. We developed and tested a number of different concepts but due to preconceptions of Telstra, feedback suggested we risked our messages being interpreted as disingenuous. What became very obvious was the need to humanise Telstra for potential employees.

Through our research we were privileged to meet and hear from some amazing people who have achieved incredible things in their careers at Telstra. We in fact have a diverse workforce; with corporate success stories, Olympians, working mothers with four children under ten, dedicated employees with more than fifty years service, ambitious graduates, indigenous employees, employees from many ethnic and social backgrounds, people who commute four hours a day just to work here, and much more. We took the view that we have more than 35,000 unique and inspiring employees and it was obvious they were the ones that needed to tell the story.

This is now the foundation of our employment brand. We describe employment opportunities at Telstra through the stories, images and videos of our own people. This provides real evidence to the claims we are making and they bring our employee value proposition to life. Our imagery is real, our people are warm and genuine, and their testimonials create a greater intimacy between our audience and the organisation.

We now have 129 employment ambassadors (and many more unofficial ambassadors) right across the country, in all parts and at all levels of the organisation. We found they were very passionate about aspects of their careers, and they constantly spoke about all the things they loved: "I love the challenging work I do", "I love the people I work with", "I love working with leading edge technology", "I love the flexibility"…..these are just some of the true testimonials from our people.

Since initial development in 2008 we have evolved our employment brand due to a common theme that emerged from the voices of our people. The internal genesis of the brand provided the basis for the new brand promise of: **A career at Telstra enables you to connect with what you love.**

So what do we do with it?

An employee value proposition and employment brand is not a nice slide pack that gets presented to senior leadership, or a page on our intranet site. An employee value proposition is the message we must use in all of our employment related communications. It forms the basis of a job ad, it allows us to decide what information we include on our careers website. It's what the recruiters tell candidates in an interview. It's what we'll align our human capital investments with, and it's also the reason our people will stay. So to be credible, all communication of the employee value proposition must be consistent – and we must deliver on the promise.

A number of new initiatives have been launched and refined to support our employer brand and enable us to attract, develop, reward and retain our employees. Some initiatives include a careers website and blog containing an in-depth video library and profiles of our people, an onboarding website, social media platforms, employer branding campaigns across integrated platforms, targeted short term campaigns for high volume and hard to fill areas, and staff direct mail campaigns. The core components of the employer brand have also become the basis for a wide range of marketing materials and HR/ recruitment communications. We have been steadfast in our commitment to always leading with the story of our ambassadors in these materials.

Measures of success

We've come a long way in four years, but there is still so much more we can achieve. In 2010 we were awarded the Fairfax Employment Marketing Award for 'Best Employment Brand', and in 2011 we're finalists in three categories.

Internally, we measure our success on a number of factors including:

- Increase in percentage of roles filled internally
- Decrease in time to fill
- Increase in the number of applications via our careers website
- Decrease job board and print ad spend

- Increase in percentage of roles filled through talent pools

Evolution in the way we attract and select

The recruitment world is changing and the way we attract and recruit employees into our organisation has changed dramatically in the past decade. Gone are the days where all you needed to do was place an ad in the early general news section of a newspaper to fill critical roles. Skills are in short supply, candidates are smart and the good ones don't need to look for a job.

So, instead of "posting and praying", recruiters are now "social recruiting" and using tools like LinkedIn, Twitter and Facebook to source passive candidates. Employee referrals are now more important than ever, as they've become the number one job source in the ICT industry - so we need to be smarter when developing sourcing strategies.

Our future areas of focus

To ensure we are remaining competitive as an organisation we need to take a huge leap and move recruitment out of its comfort zone. No longer are we able to rely on recruiting active candidates when unemployment is virtually non-existent.

A key focus for those of us addressing this issue will be identifying top talent and developing sourcing strategies that allow us to reach these candidates who are not actively seeking work. In order to do this we need to build high quality talent pools via sourcing, social recruiting, talent mapping and online talent communities – and consistently reinforce the real opportunities and benefits available to individuals though our employment brand message. The talent communities will provide opportunities for engagement, knowledge sharing and two-way conversations. The challenge will be in developing compelling and rich content in a user-friendly portal where people will want to return on a frequent basis.

The continual improvement of our employment brand strategy is now more important than ever, as we need to ensure all of our communications through these new mediums are consistent. As attempts to communicate our employee value proposition simply through photos, headlines and copy in a newspaper ad are no longer particularly effective, we need to be creative with how this message is delivered. This is why the development of communication strategies, in-depth sourcing strategies and social media recruiting strategies are now necessary in the employment brand space. We need to be constantly challenging the status quo and looking for better ways to do things, at what new technologies will enable us to do and what innovative tools and ideas we can adopt.

Another area of key importance is the continual development of our employee value proposition and employment brand so it is strategically aligned, competitively different and reflecting the reality of our organization - today and in the future. Obviously there will always be a slightly aspirational element to an employee value proposition, as individuals vary and not everyone is enjoying the same employment experience, or is as engaged as the person next to them. But, the risk of communicating the wrong messages or not actually delivering on the employee value proposition will clearly affect our engagement and retention rates.

In an organisation of our size, the segmentation of our employee value proposition is another way to recognise the diverse interests and talents of our people and what is most important to them in a career. We have just completed an employment brand and employee value proposition for women, and we are now looking at the different functions within our business to identify whether our employee value proposition resonates with them - or may need fine tuning for their particular segments. This will enable us to take the right message to market and ultimately convince them to consider Telstra as an employer of choice in that segment.

Employment communications and the recruitment industry have responded to many challenges in the last few years and have rapidly evolved to keep up. Five years ago employee value propositions and employment brands were buzzwords and common only to large organisations. It is astonishing how fast this space is moving, so it is exciting to imagine what the next five years will bring.

Brie Macklin, Employment Brand Manager, Telstra

Aligning the sun, the moon and the stars

Aligning internally to achieve external outcomes

Alison McLeod – Ernst & Young

Ernst & Young reflect on their employer branding strategy and provide a roadmap to ignite stakeholder engagement and passion.

Ernst & Young is a $24 billion global organisation, operating in 140 countries. Its 141,000 people work across offices in 650 cities and provide 300,000 client accounts with advisory, assurance, transactions and tax services.

Professional services firms like Ernst & Young are structured uniquely when compared to other organisations. Based on a partnership model, Ernst & Young partners run their business units as individual companies. Leadership is provided at a global, area, sub-area level, across distinct business service lines.

As one of the 'big four' global professional services firms, Ernst & Young has a strong corporate brand, and its brand reputation and leading people culture are important to candidates. However, Ernst & Young recognise that in a talent competitive market, they shouldn't assume that a candidate understands what makes Ernst & Young a great employer or what a career at Ernst & Young would be like.

That's why the firm is committed to continually improving its people culture and building a unique employer brand by communicating to candidates the many ways that Ernst & Young is a great place to work.

Our initial approach

Ernst & Young has a great story to tell. Through research, we know we deliver employment experiences that our employees want; however our highly complex organisation – a matrix structure integrating geography and business service lines - means that we face three key challenges when formulating an employer brand strategy:

1. The variety of partner operating styles and sub-cultures within specific business service lines and geographies means that employment experiences can vary considerably across the firm.
2. Our competitors for talent largely offer the same employment experience to candidates and employees, and actively communicate their offering to candidates.
3. Distinct business service lines have historically led to a degree of cannibalisation across the firm. Fragmentation of overarching firm-wide messages creates confusion for both candidates and employees.

Faced with these challenges, we asked ourselves three core questions:

1. What employment experiences are consistent across Ernst & Young firm-wide?
2. What misconceptions need to be addressed in the short to mid-term to change how people perceive Ernst & Young (internally and externally)?

3. What are the proof points, or core tangible outcomes that each business service line delivers that can be communicated through a common set of firm-wide experiences?

These questions helped to shape our thinking; about how to move the employer brand research findings from strategy to reality. We asked ourselves how we could begin turning data into a communication framework that would be easily understood and supported across the firm.

To analyse the research findings, we developed the following model:

- Global: Achieving your potential – Overarching employer brand positioning
- Sub-Area: How do we help people achieve their potential in Australia and New Zealand? – Generic Employee Value Proposition themes
- Service Line: What do we promise to deliver at service line level? – Specific proof points

At every level within the firm, our people receive directives telling them what to do and what to say. Therefore creating a communication strategy that clearly shows how all the messages are connected was critical to engage the business.

To cut through internal noise and engage people, we constructed a message hierarchy that illustrated how messages relate to the global employer brand position, how they work at a firm-wide level to provide consistency and how proof points at a business service line level deliver on our employment promise.

Getting started

Once we determined what we wanted to change and how we wanted to change; we faced the dilemma of who to tell and where to start. Given a recent restructuring within the firm, we decided to take a grass root, bottom-up approach by first educating our recruitment and HR operations teams. These teams connect directly with partners and senior leaders within their respective business service lines, and collectively support a diverse range of 'people' requirements. They are key primary influencers both internally and externally so it was particularly important to 'bring employer branding' to life for these two teams.

Our first course of action was to dispel the myths about what employer branding is and isn't, and help our recruitment and HR operations teams understand how effective employer branding can achieve strategic outcomes. This education process also proved to be an effective way to engage these teams and secure buy-in. With five different business service lines operating across recruitment and HR, engaging these teams was critical to the successful launch of the program.

So how did we do this? We conducted a series of interactive employer branding master classes that were tailored to business service lines. These master classes highlighted the key milestones in our roadmap, and provided the teams with three main takeaways:

1. Firm-wide messages give us consistency. It means we can all promote the 'same' firm-side set of reasons why Ernst & Young is a great place to work.

2. There are certain messages we need to prioritise in the short-term to change the misconceptions that candidates and our people have about Ernst & Young.
3. At a business service line level, we needed to research the stories that would provide evidence to support these messages.

While we recognised that employer branding isn't a solution that can be delivered at a click of a finger; we knew that there were quick wins we could achieve to address candidate misconceptions about Ernst & Young. We knew we needed to give our HR operations team time to set longer term goals at a granular business service line level.

Recruiters were hungry to put the messages into practice and begin addressing the misconceptions in the market - so we equipped them with the tools to help them do this. We developed briefing sheets, interview guidelines and advertising toolkits customised to experienced-hire needs and replicated a set of materials to support campus recruitment needs. Recruitment messaging was consistent across all candidate positions - from experienced hires to student level engagements; however we also briefed our teams about when to appropriately adjust certain themes depending on the target audience. For instance, a message about 'meaningful work' means something very different to an experienced candidate versus a graduate. At a graduate level, meaningful work is about being able to use the skills and knowledge they have gained from their degree; for an experienced hire, meaningful work is about the extent to which a solution has impacted a client's business or decision making process.

Engaging the leadership of the firm

While the recruiters were busy addressing candidates' misconceptions about Ernst & Young, the HR operations team kicked off discussions internally with partners and senior leaders. In a firm like Ernst & Young, the best results come from collaboration and building ownership across the firm's leadership team.

This is only possible if decision-makers feel part of the process. Not only does it simply make good business sense - those in the business know their business best - but it also engages and empowers stakeholders from the outset. There is a tendency to keep employer branding research under lock and key and not to share information or be transparent with the wider organisation. There is also a tendency to work with an external agency to develop creative and copy and then only engage the business when the end-product is signed, sealed and delivered. At which stage, it is often too late to incorporate their input.

At Ernst & Young, it was critical not to dictate to the business what the employer brand was, but rather to involve leaders and have them shape what the employer brand could be. Given our structure, we embarked on a five pronged, simultaneous approach. Each HR operations leader steered their partner group to work through and agree on firm-wide messages and apply the research findings relevant to their business service line. Each group identified the current employment experiences of their people, areas for improvement and what new practices and experiences they wanted to develop in the future.

We encouraged our HR operations teams to focus on four or five key priorities and get these right, rather than overstretch their budgets and resources in an attempt to achieve everything. We also provided guidance to ensure that their key priorities were aligned with their business's objectives. HR practitioners often warn against using aspirational messaging. However, we believe that as long as there is leadership commitment and a plan to deliver on the promise, then including aspirational messaging can be effectively leveraged to help differentiate employment experiences in the marketplace.

Although each business service line started this program at the same time, arriving at the initial milestone of having finalised lists of proof points, defining corresponding messages and having agreed priorities with their partners, has been quite staggered. Ideally it would have been more efficient in the short term to impose deadlines on this part of the process however by being flexible with timing we were able to secure the best results to build a solid foundation for our employer brand.

In addition, we did not expect our HR team to be employer brand experts, nor did we expect our employer branding team to be versed on the finer nuances of HR - but by providing guidance, showing direction, sharing key learnings from across the different teams and acting as a silent third party in the process, we created synergies across team competencies to deliver results.

Next steps

So, what lies ahead? Our next step is to road test the messages to ensure that they resonate with employees. This will comprise employee focus groups that will check that our messaging appropriately reflects actual employee experiences.

Following this final test stage, we will then bring our recruitment and HR operations teams back together again to update us on their key outcomes, and our HR operations team will roll-out a series of initiatives at different levels in the firm to engage our people about what it means to be part of Ernst & Young.

In summary, to develop a global employer brand position across a complex matrix business requires considerable internal coordination and a flexible communications framework that accommodates individual service line business objectives while also providing unifying firm-wide messages and themes.

Ernst & Young's leading people culture continues to evolve. By strategically aligning ourselves internally we are finding we are can better engage with our external candidate audiences.

Alison McLeod | Oceania Recruitment Leader | PEO-Recruiting, Ernst & Young

Lightning Source UK Ltd.
Milton Keynes UK
UKOW04f1133080414

229591UK00002B/61/P

9 781742 841342